The Organization of the Church

By

John Isaac Edwards

Truth
Publications ™

ISBN 10: 158427-321-6

ISBN 13: 978-1-58427-321-9

Truth Publications
CEI Bookstore
220 S. Marion St., Athens, AL 35611
855-492-6657
sales@truthpublications.com

Table of Contents

The Organization of the Church

We welcome you to this series of Bible studies concerning the organization of the Lord's church. It is the purpose of these lessons to assist truth seekers and growing Christians in a better understanding of the organization of the church as revealed on the pages of the New Testament.

Please take your Bible, look up the Scriptures listed, fill in the blanks where called for, and answer any questions. These lessons are based on the King James Version of the Bible.

Paul and Timotheus, the servants of Jesus Christ, to all the saints in Christ Jesus which are at Philippi, with the bishops and deacons (Phil. 1:1).

If you have any questions or comments as you study these lessons, write them down so you can remember to mention them at the right time and place. Write your name on your material as you will want to keep it for future study.

Name: _____

Date and Place of Study:_____

Material Prepared By:
John Isaac Edwards

Introduction: Learning About Church Organization

Introduction

1. The Scriptures furnish us with a plan for the organization of the Lord's church.
2. A study of the organization of the church is of utmost importance for now and for the generations to come.

Discussion

I. The Need for This Study

    A. Let's notice some reasons why a study of the organization of the church is needed.

        1. *To declare all the counsel of God.* We are obligated to declare "all the counsel of God" (Acts 20:27). God has given counsel concerning how the church is to be organized. To neglect teaching on the organization of the church is to shun to declare all the counsel of God.

        2. *To help each member know his place.* God expects His people to be in their place (Judg. 7:21). Each member of the church has a place in the organization of the church. The only way we can know our place is by study.

        3. *To encourage young men to become qualified leaders.* Young men must be trained to become qualified leaders in the church. It takes time and hard work to be qualified for a position of leadership in the church. A church would do well to keep some kind of training program ongoing to help train such.

4. *To strengthen the church.* The stronger the organization of the church, the stronger the church. Poor leadership retards the growth of the church.
5. *To clear up misunderstanding.* The organization of the church has been misunderstood by many. The only way to clear up misunderstanding is by clearly teaching the truth as it is revealed on the pages of divine inspiration.
6. *To prevent apostasy.* The apostasy of Israel was brought about by changing God's form of organization (1 Sam. 8:1-6). Most apostasies in the church have begun within the organization of the church (Acts 20:28-30; 2 Thess. 2:2-4).

B. As long as the church exists, there will be a great need to study its organization.

II. The Definition of Organization

A. *Webster's Unabridged Dictionary* defines the word "organization" as: "1. The act of organizing; the act or process of arranging and getting into proper working order; as, the organization of an expedition. 2. The state of being organized; that which is organized; an organized body. 3. Organic structure; the disposition or arrangement of the organs for the performance of vital functions. 4. The arrangement of the parts of an aggregate or body for work or action; systematic preparation for action."

B. Some New Testament passages which set forth the concept of organization:
1. 1 Corinthians 11:34—". . .And the rest will I set in _____ when I come."
2. 1 Corinthians 14:40—"Let all things be done _____ and in _____."
3. Titus 1:5—". . . that thou shouldest set in _____ the things that are wanting..."

C. The organization of the church is the arrangement of the parts of the body for the accomplishment of the work God has given the church to do.

III. The Importance of Organization

A. Where there is no organization, there is chaos and disorder!

B. Organization is important for order and accomplishment when two or more people are associated in any given task.

C. The lack of good organization is one of the greatest hindrances to efficiently accomplishing the work God has given the church to do.

IV. The Term "Church" as Used in the New Testament

A. The term "church" is used in two senses in the New Testament.
   1. *Universal sense.* The universal church includes all of the Lord's people everywhere. The term "church" is used in a universal sense in such passages as Matthew 16:18; Acts 2:47.
   2. *Local sense.* The local church includes the Lord's people in a definite geographical location. The term "church" is used in a local sense in such passages as Acts 13:1; 1 Corinthians 1:2; 1 Thessalonians 1:1.
B. There is no organization of the church on earth in a universal sense. God has given organization to the local church. Organizations larger or smaller than the local church are without divine authority.

V. The Autonomy of the Local Church

A. The word "autonomy" is defined as, "independent in government; self-governing; without outside control" (*Webster's International Dictionary*).
B. God gave to the local church the right of self-government.
   1. The Bible calls for elders in every church (Acts 14:23; Titus 1:5). The authority of elders is limited to the local church (Acts 20:28; 1 Pet. 5:2).
   2. Each church does its own work under the supervision of its own elders.
      a. The local church sent out preachers (Acts 11:22).
      b. The local church supported preachers laboring in foreign fields (Phil. 4:15-18).
      c. The local church made up its own funds for relief (1 Cor. 16:1-3; Acts 11:27-30).
      d. The local church selected and sent its own messengers with its funds for the work to be done (1 Cor. 16:1-4; 2 Cor. 8:4-6, 16-21).
C. Each local church is to be organized the same way; directed by the same Head; are each charged to do the same work; and are to function independent of each other — not through each other.

VI. The Sufficiency of the Church

    A. The church is fully equipped to do all that the Lord has given it to do (Eph. 4:7-16).

    B. No other organization is permitted, much less needed.

    C. Our trouble today is not a lack of sufficient organization, but a failure to use what the Lord has provided!

VII. The Organization of the Church in a Nutshell

    A. Christ is the absolute authority in the local church (Eph. 1:21-23).

    B. Christ gave apostles, prophets, evangelists, pastors and teachers to make the church sufficient and function as a whole for His purpose (Eph. 4:9-16).

    C. Paul wrote the Philippian letter, ". . . to all the _____ in Christ Jesus which are at Philippi, with the _____ and _____" (Phil. 1:1).

Conclusion

1. We should be content with God's pattern for the organization of the church.

2. Let's keep the church pure in organization!

    The Organization of the Church

Christ: Head of the Church

Introduction
1. No organization or body can long exist without a head.
2. In the church, Jesus Christ is the Head and in all things has the pre-eminence (Col. 1:18).

Discussion

I.   Christ Has All Authority in Heaven and Earth
    A. What did Christ claim in Matthew 28:18?_____

    _____
    B. Who gave Christ all authority (1 Cor. 15:23-28; Eph. 1:17-23)?

    _____
    C. Christ taught as one having _____ (Matt. 7:29).
    D. If Christ has all authority (and He does), how much authority does that leave for us in religious matters? _____

II. All Things Are to Be Done in the Name of Christ
    A. The Scriptures admonish us to do all by the authority of Jesus Christ.
    B. Paul wrote, "And whatsoever ye do in _____ or _____, do all in the _____ of the Lord Jesus, giving thanks to God and the Father by him" (Col. 3:17).
    C. We must have a "thus saith the Lord" for all that we say and do!

III. Passages Which Set Forth Christ as Head of the Church
    A. Many passages after Matthew 28:18 show Christ to be the Head of the church.
       1. Ephesians 1:22—"And hath put all things under his feet, and gave him to be the _____ over all things to the _____."
       2. Ephesians 4:15—"But speaking the truth in love, may grow

up into him in all things, which is the _____, even
_____."

3. Ephesians 5:23—"For the husband is the head of the
   wife, even as _____ is the _____ of the
   _____."

4. Colossians 1:18—"And he is the _____ of the body, the
   _____, who is the beginning, the firstborn from the
   dead; that in all things he might have the preeminence."

B. There can be no other head of the church than Jesus Christ, the
   Son of God!

IV. Every Figure of the Church Pictures the Preeminence of Christ

A. The church is set forth in the New Testament in many figures.
   There is no feature of the church that does not picture Christ as
   the absolute authority. As you study some of the figures of the
   church, fill in the blanks and answer any questions.

1. *High Priest.* The Lord's people are a "chosen generation, a
   royal _____" (1 Pet. 2:9). Each member of the
   church is a priest and offers up spiritual sacrifices (1 Pet.
   2:5). According to Hebrews 3:1, who is the High Priest?

   _____

2. *Chief Corner Stone.* The church of Christ is a spiritual house
   (1 Tim. 3:15). Peter taught, "Ye also, as lively stones, are
   built up a spiritual _____" (1 Pet. 2:5). Who is the
   Chief Corner Stone (1 Pet. 2:6)? _____

3. *Chief Shepherd.* Each child of God is a sheep in God's flock
   (1 Pet. 5:2). Who is pictured as the Chief Shepherd (1 Pet.
   5:4)?_____

4. *Captain.* When we become members of the church, we are
   enlisted in the army of the Lord (2 Tim. 2:3-4). Who is pictured as the Captain of this mighty army (Heb. 2:10)?

   _____

5. *Bridegroom.* Members of the church are married to Christ
   (Rom. 7:1-4). The church is described as the bride of Christ
   (2 Cor. 11:2). Thus, the church wears the name of Christ
   (Acts 11:26; Rom. 16:16) and must be faithful in all things
   (Eph. 1:1; 5:22-25). Who is the Bridegroom (John 3:29)?

   _____

6. *King.* The church is set forth as a kingdom (Matt. 16:16-19). Who does the Bible teach is the King (1 Tim. 6:15; 1 Cor. 15:24-27)? _____

7. *Vine.* When the church is set forth as a vineyard, and individual saints are represented as branches, who is the Vine (John 15:1-10)? _____

B. What conclusion can be drawn from these figures of the church?

_____

_____

V. The Headquarters of the Church

A. The headquarters of the church is where the Head is. Read the following passages and note where Christ is found.

1. Acts 2:32-36 _____

2. Acts 7:55-56 _____

3. Ephesians 6:9 _____

4. Hebrews 9:24 _____

5. 1 Peter 3:21-22 _____

B. Now, in light of these passages, where is the headquarters of the church? _____

Conclusion

1. In the church, Christ is the absolute authority and He rules through the written word.

2. We must always be in submission to the law of Christ (Gal. 6:2).

Lesson 3

Apostles and Prophets: Foundation of the Church

Introduction

1. God set apostles and prophets in the church (1 Cor. 12:28).
2. The apostles and prophets pertained to the foundation of the church (Eph. 2:19-20).

Discussion

I. Apostles

    A. The word "apostle" means one sent, and is applied to different persons in the New Testament.

        1. "Apostle" is used of Christ, the _____ of God (Heb. 3:1). In what sense is Christ called an apostle (John 17:3)?

        _____

        2. "Apostle" is used of men chosen and sent out by the Lord to preach the gospel (Matt. 10:1-5).

        3. "Apostle" is used of messengers chosen by churches and sent out on special errands (2 Cor. 8:23; Phil. 2:25).

    B. List the names of the apostles of Christ (Matt. 10:2-4; Acts 1:26; 14:14; Gal. 1:1): _____

      _____

      _____

      _____

    C. The qualifications of the apostles of Christ.

        1. *Had to be with Christ from the beginning* (John 15:26-27; Acts 1:21-22). Who was the exception to this qualification (1 Cor. 15:8)?_____

2. *Had to be an eyewitness of the resurrection of Christ from the dead; had to have seen the Lord* (Matt. 26:32; 28:7; Acts 1:22; 26:16; 1 Cor. 9:1; 15:5-8).
3. *Had to be chosen by Christ* (Acts 1:2; Matt. 10:1-5; Acts 1:24; Gal. 1:1).
4. Are there apostles in the church today? _____

D. The authority of the apostles of Christ.
1. Christ "gave them _____ and _____ over all devils, and to cure diseases" (Luke 9:1).
2. The apostles were given _____ and _____ power (Matt. 16:19; 18:18).
3. The apostles were given power after the Holy Spirit came upon them (Acts 1:8; 2:1-4). The Holy Spirit guided the apostles into all _____ (John 16:13).
4. The authority of the apostles was universal in scope, in that their power extended over all the churches equally (2 Cor. 11:28).

E. The signs of the apostles of Christ.
1. 2 Corinthians 12:12
2. List some signs of an apostle. _____
_____
_____
3. Signs distinguished true apostles from "false apostles" (2 Cor. 11:13).

F. The work of the apostles of Christ.
1. The work of the apostles involved laying the ground work for the Lord's church (Eph. 2:19-20).
2. The apostles were ambassadors of Christ (2 Cor. 5:20; Eph. 6:20). What is an ambassador? _____
_____
To receive or reject such an envoy is to receive or reject the one who sent him (Luke 10:16; John 13:20).
3. The apostles revealed the will of Christ to men (Gal. 1:15-16).
4. The apostles serve as judges (Matt. 19:28). In what way are the apostles judges?_____

II. Prophets
A. A "prophet" is "one who speaks forth. In the New Testament,

one who, moved by the Spirit of God and hence his organ or spokesman, solemnly declares to men what he has received by inspiration, esp. future events, and in particular such as relate to the cause and kingdom of God and to human salvation" (Thayer, *Greek-English Lexicon of the New Testament*).

  B. The selection and qualifications of New Testament prophets.

    1. Selected among males and females (Acts 2:17-18; 21:8-10; 1 Cor. 11:4-5).

    2. Chosen and qualified by the Lord (Acts 2:17-18), or through laying on of an apostle's hands (Acts 19:6-7).

  C. The functions of the prophets.

    1. The functions of the prophets involved laying the ground work for the Lord's church (Eph. 2:19-20).

    2. The prophets predicted future events (Acts 11:27-28; 21:10-11).

    3. The prophets revealed the counsels and purposes of the Heavenly Father (Eph. 3:4-5; 1 Cor. 2:7-16).

    4. The prophets distinguished between the inspired word of God and the uninspired teachings of men (1 Cor. 14:37).

    5. The prophets exhorted, confirmed, and edified the Lord's church (1 Cor. 14:3, 31).

    6. The prophets convicted the unbeliever of sin and constrained him to worship God (1 Cor. 14:23-24).

  D. The prophetic office was temporary (1 Cor. 13:8-13).

  E. Christians had to beware of "false prophets" (Acts 13:6; 2 Pet. 2:1; 1 John 4:1).

Conclusion

1. The apostles and prophets were among the gifts given by the Lord to make the church sufficient and function as a whole for His purpose.

2. The apostolic and prophetic offices came to an end when revelation was complete.

Evangelists: Gospel Preachers (1)

Introduction
1. The Lord gave evangelists to the organization of the church (Eph. 4: 11).
2. The primary responsibility of evangelists is gospel preaching (2 Tim. 4:1-5).

Discussion
I. **Scriptural Designations of Evangelists**
 A. *Preacher* (1 Tim. 2:7; 2 Tim. 1:11; Rom. 10:14). The word "preacher" means "a herald" (Vine, *Expository Dictionary of New Testament Words*). "Preacher" tells what one does: proclaims a message.
 B. *Evangelist* (2 Tim. 4:5; Eph. 4:11-12; Acts 21:8). "Evangelist" refers to "a messenger of good" (Vine, *Expository Dictionary of New Testament Words*). "This name is given in the New Testament to those heralds of salvation through Christ who are not apostles" (Thayer, *Greek-English Lexicon of the New Testament*). An evangelist is one who brings the good news of the gospel concerning the way of salvation (Rom. 10:15). "Evangelist" tells the nature of one's message: good news, glad tidings.
 C. *Minister* (Eph. 3:7; Col. 1:23, 25; 1 Tim. 4:6). The word "minister" means a servant or attendant. "Minister" describes his relationship to what he does: he is a servant, not a master. He is a spiritual minister or servant (Acts 6:2).

II. **Evangelists and Religious Titles**
 A. Some refer to evangelists in improper and unscriptural ways. Here are some examples:

1. *Reverend.* God alone is Reverend (Psa. 111:9).
2. *Father.* No man is to be called "father" in a religious sense (Matt. 23:9).
3. *Pastor.* The elders are the pastors of the church (Eph. 4:11-12).

B. What is the message of Job 32:21-22 and Matthew 23:8-12?

_____

_____

III. The Qualifications of an Evangelist

A. Do you ever read of women evangelists in the New Testament (Acts 21:8; 2 Tim. 4:5)?

B. There are basically two qualifications of an evangelist: *faithful* and *able* (2 Tim. 2:2). Write a few words explaining what these terms mean.

1. Faithful. _____

_____

2. Able. _____

_____

IV. The Work of an Evangelist

A. Writing Timothy, Paul said, "do the _____ of an _____ " (2 Tim. 4:5).

B. The primary work of an evangelist is preaching the gospel.

1. 2 Timothy 4:2—" _____ the _____; be instant in season, out of season; reprove, rebuke, exhort with all longsuffering and doctrine."

2. 1 Corinthians 9:16—"For though I _____ the _____, I have nothing to glory of: for necessity is laid upon me; yea, woe is unto me, if I preach not the gospel."

C. Discuss the importance of the evangelist's work. _____

_____

_____

V. The Authority of an Evangelist

A. Is the expression "evangelistic authority" found in the Bible?

_____

B. Paul told Titus, "These things speak, and exhort, and rebuke with all _____ " (Titus 2:15).

C. An evangelist must do only as the word of God commands. He has no authority within his own office.

VI. Learning from Philip, the Evangelist
    A. Read Acts 8 and learn some things about Philip, the evangelist (Acts 21:8).
        1. Philip preached Christ (Acts 8:5).
        2. Philip preached the basics (Acts 8:12).
        3. Philip was obedient (Acts 8:27).
        4. Philip was enthusiastic (Acts 8:30).
        5. Philip found where folks were in their understanding (Acts 8:30).
        6. Philip opened his mouth (Acts 8:35).
    B. We need more evangelists today like Philip, the evangelist!

VII. Lessons Evangelists Can Learn from Paul
    A. Evangelists would do well to study the life and preaching of Paul.
        1. *Paul was consistent.*
            a. Paul taught the same thing in every church (1 Cor. 4:17; 7:17).
            b. Many evangelists are inconsistent. Truth is always consistent!
        2. *Paul was not ashamed of the gospel of Christ.*
            a. Romans 1:16-17
            b. Many today seem to be ashamed of the gospel in their preaching.
        3. *Paul was simple.*
            a. 1 Corinthians 2:1-7
            b. 2 Corinthians 11:3
            c. There is too much "over-the-head" preaching today.
        4. *Paul was humble.*
            a. Acts 20:19
            b. Too many evangelists display a haughty attitude.
        5. *Paul preached to please God.*
            a. Galatians 1:10
            b. The success of a preacher is not measured by the accolades of men.
        6. *Paul practiced what he preached.*
            a. Paul showed them and taught them (Acts 20:20).

        b.   The life of an evangelist must be in harmony with his preaching.

        c.   What does Romans 2:21-22 have to say about this? ____

_____

_____

   B. Evangelists should strive to pattern themselves after the example of Paul.

Conclusion

1.   The work of evangelists pertains to the extension of the church, and is of great importance.

2.   Discuss why you think there is a shortage of faithful, able evangelists today.

Evangelists: Gospel Preachers (2)

Introduction

1. We continue to study the place of evangelists in the organization of the church.
2. In this lesson, we will notice some responsibilities of evangelists, the "located" evangelist issue, and the support of an evangelist.

Discussion

I. Some Responsibilities of Evangelists

  A. The books of 1 and 2 Timothy and Titus were written to evangelists and record some responsibilities of evangelists. Let's observe some.

    1. *Responsibilities to self.*
        a. "_____ thyself rather unto godliness" (1 Tim. 4:7).
        b. "_____ _____ unto thyself" (1 Tim. 4:16).
        c. "_____ thyself _____" (1 Tim. 5:22).
        d. "_____ in the grace that is in Christ Jesus" (2 Tim. 2:1).
        e. "_____ also youthful lusts: but _____ righteousness, faith, charity, peace" (2 Tim. 2:22).

    2. *Responsibilities to the brethren.*
        a. ". . . Put the brethren in _____" (1 Tim. 4:6).
        b. ". . . Be thou an _____ of the believers" (1 Tim. 4:12).
        c. "Rebuke not an elder, but intreat him as a _____; and the younger men as _____; The elder

women as _____; the younger as
_____. . . . Honour _____. . ." (1 Tim.
5:1-2).

d. "_____ them that are _____ in this
world" (1 Tim. 6:17).

e. ". . . The things that thou hast heard _____ _____. . .
_____ thou to faithful men, who shall be able to
teach others also" (2 Tim. 2:2).

f. "In meekness _____ those that oppose
themselves..." (2 Tim. 2:25).

3. *Responsibilities to elders.*

a. "Let the elders that rule well be counted worthy of
double _____. . ." (1 Tim. 5:17).

b. "Against an elder receive not an _____, but
before two or three witnesses" (1 Tim. 5:19).

c. "Them that sin _____ before all. . ." (1 Tim. 5:20).

d. ". . . Doing nothing by _____" (1 Tim. 5:21).

e. "Lay _____ suddenly on no man. . ." (1 Tim. 5:22).

4. *Responsibilities to the gospel.*

a. "These things _____ and _____"
(1 Tim. 4:11).

b. "_____ upon these things; give thyself
wholly to them. . ." (1 Tim. 4:15).

c. "Be not thou therefore _____ of the
testimony of our Lord, nor of me his prisoner. . ." (2
Tim. 1:8).

d. ". . . Be thou _____ of the afflictions of the
gospel" (2 Tim. 1:8).

5. *Responsibilities to the church.*

a. ". . . Set in _____ the things that are wanting"
(Titus 1:5).

b. ". . . _____ elders" (Titus 1:5).

6. *Responsibilities to false teachers.*

a. ". . . From such _____thyself" (1 Tim. 6:5).

b. ". . . From such _____ away" (2 Tim. 3:5).

c. "Whose mouths must be _____. . ." (Titus 1:11).

d. ". . . _____ them sharply. . ." (Titus 1:13).

e. "A man that is an heretick after the first and second admonition _______________" (Titus 3:10).

B. This should help us appreciate that evangelists have tremendous responsibility.

II. The "Located" Evangelist Issue

A. Some say it is unscriptural for an evangelist to be located. That is, he cannot stay at one place for a very long period of time.

B. The Bible teaches an evangelist may stay in one area as long as there is the work of an evangelist to be done.

1. Barnabas and Paul were located at Antioch for 1 year (Acts 11:26).
2. Paul was located at Corinth for 1 ½ years (Acts 18:11).
3. Paul was located at Ephesus for 3 years (Acts 20:31).
4. Luke was located at Philippi for 7 - 8 years (Acts 16:10-17:1; 20:6).
5. Philip was at Ceasarea for 20 years, it is estimated.

III. The Support of an Evangelist

A. An evangelist has the right to work and support himself (Acts 18:1-3).

B. An evangelist has the right to be financially supported by the church (1 Cor. 9:4-14; 2 Cor. 11:8; Phil. 1:3-5; 4:10-16).

C. An evangelist has the right to be supported by individual Christians (Gal. 6:6-10; 1 Cor. 16:17-18).

Conclusion

1. Discuss what we can do to encourage men to want to become evangelists.
2. Discuss some things a preacher needs.

Lesson 6

Elders: Shepherds of the Flock (1)

Introduction

1. God has ordained that elders be appointed in every church (Acts 14:23; Titus 1:5).
2. The responsibility of elders involves being shepherds of the flock. Peter, writing to elders, said, "Feed the flock of God which is among you..." (1 Pet. 5:1-2).

Discussion

I. Descriptive Terms Designating the Office of Elders

    A. There are three different terms in the Bible used to designate the office of elders.

        1. *Elder* (*presbuteros*). The term "elder" means one advanced in life, a senior. This describes the individual in terms of dignity and experience (1 Pet. 5:1).

        2. *Bishop* (*episkopos*). The term "bishop" means an overseer, watcher, guardian, or superintendent. "Bishop" describes him in terms of his funtion as one overseeing (1 Tim. 3:1-2; Phil. 1:1).

        3. *Pastor* (*poimen*). The term "pastor" means herdsman or shepherd and portrays him as tending the Lord's sheep (Eph. 4:11).

    B. Show that these terms all refer to the same office or group of men (Acts 20:17, 28; Titus 1:5, 7; 1 Pet. 5:1-2). _____

_____

_____

II. The Number of Men to Serve as Elders

A. Read the following passages and note whether the Bible teaches a singular number of elders or a plurality of elders over one congregation.
   1. Acts 11:30 _____
   2. Acts 14:23 _____
   3. Acts 20:17, 28 _____
   4. Titus 1:5, 7 _____
   5. 1 Peter 5:1-2 _____

B. What about one man overseeing the congregation as the elder?
   _____
   _____

C. Since there is a plurality of elders, it is imperative that elders work together.

III. The Authority of Elders

A. That elders have authority none can really deny, but some elders abuse their authority.

B. Elders do not have unlimited authority. For example, elders cannot make laws since Christ is the lawgiver (Jas. 4:12). Neither can they change laws!

C. How does 1 Peter 5:1-3 limit the authority of elders? _____
   _____

D. Elders need to agree. One elder is not in a position to make decisions for the eldership. He is out of place when this is done.

IV. Some False Concepts Concerning Elders

A. *No elders.*
   1. There are some who teach that there should be no elders at all.
   2. Some reason that the eldership passed away with spiritual gifts.
   3. Show authority from the Bible for elders. _____
      _____
   4. List some reasons why you think there would be some who do not want any elders in the church. _____
      _____
      _____

B. *Men may just assume the eldership.*
   1. Some think that maybe men of social prominence or financial success will just assume the office of an elder.

The Organization of the Church ⸻⸻⸻⸻⸻⸻⸻ 23

      2. What is wrong with this concept? _____

  C. *Evangelistic oversight.*
      1. Some want to put the evangelist in charge.
      2. The Bible makes a distinction between *elders* (pastors) and *evangelists* (Eph. 4:11).
  D. *Grow into qualifications after appointed.*
      1. 1 Timothy 3:2—"A bishop _____ must be..."
      2. Suppose he fails to grow!
  E. *Group qualifications.*
      1. The idea is that we may appoint one man with some qualifications, another man with others, and so on until all the qualifications are met (1 Tim. 3:2).
      2. We would not elect a man to public office like the Congress on this basis.

V. The Work of Elders
  A. *Elders are self-examiners.*
      1. Paul instructed elders, "Take heed therefore unto _____ _____ . . ." (Acts 20:28).
      2. The first responsibility of every elder is to himself.
  B. *Elders are example-setters.*
      1. Peter exhorted elders to be "_____ to the flock" (1 Pet. 5:3).
      2. List some ways elders can be examples to the flock. _____

  C. *Elders are overseers.*
      1. Acts 20:28
      2. Are there any limits on the oversight of elders? _____

  D. *Elders are flock-feeders.*
      1. Acts 20:28
      2. 1 Peter 5:2
      3. What does this involve? _____

  E. *Elders are soul-watchers.*
      1. Hebrews 13:17

2. How do elders watch for souls? _____

_____

F. *Elders are rulers.*
   1. 1 Timothy 3:4-5
   2. Note how elders must rule (Rom. 12:7-8; 1 Tim. 5:17).

   _____

   _____

   _____

G. List some other things involved in the work of elders. _____

   _____

   _____

   _____

H. What words in Hebrews 13:17 show the importance of the work
   of elders? _____

   _____

   _____

Conclusion
1. Elders have been given a very important and serious work.
2. We need to understand God's place for elders in the organization of
   the church.

Lesson 7

Elders: Shepherds of the Flock (2)

Introduction
1. We continue to study God's place for elders in the local church.
2. Let's notice the qualifications of elders. Please read 1 Timothy 3:1-7 and Titus 1:5-9.

Discussion

I. General Qualifications

   A. *A man* (1 Tim. 3:1). What does this do to a woman? _____
_____

   B. *Desires the office* (1 Tim. 3:1). A man must long for the work and stretch out for it.

II. Family Qualifications

   A. *Husband of one wife* (1 Tim. 3:2; Titus 1:6). Literally, "a one-woman man." This eliminates the bachelor. A man must not have more than one wife.

   B. *Rules well his own house* (1 Tim. 3:4-5). He must be able to manage his family. What is the reason for this qualification? __
_____

   C. *Having his children in subjection with all gravity* (1 Tim. 3:4). This means the children are under control (Eph. 6:1-4; Col. 3:20-21), and discipline is practiced in the home (Prov. 13:24).

   D. *Having faithful children not accused of riot or unruly* (Titus 1:6). If a man cannot influence his children to be faithful, how can he influence others? _____
_____

III. Reputation Qualification
    A. *A good report from without* (1 Tim. 3:7).
    B. A man must have a good reputation even among those who are not members of the church. It must be as Titus was told in Titus 2:8.

IV. Ability Qualifications
    A. *Apt to teach* (1 Tim. 3:2). What does this mean? _____

    _____

    This requires lots of study time (2 Tim. 2:15). Feeding the flock certainly involves teaching and seeing that the flock is properly taught (Acts 20:28).
    B. *Holding fast the faithful word and able to exhort and convince the gainsayer* (Titus 1:9). He has to know the truth so well that he can detect false doctrine early and deal with it.
    C. If a man is unable to do this, what is the danger to the local church? _____

    _____

    _____

V. Experience Qualification
    A. *Not a novice* (1 Tim. 3:6).
    B. What is a novice? _____

    _____

    C. What reason is given for this qualification? _____

    _____

    _____

VI. Negative Qualifications
    A. *Not given to wine* (1 Tim. 3:3; Titus 1:7). A man must possess certain qualities of character to be an elder. An elder who drinks sets a bad example.
    B. *No striker* (1 Tim. 3:3; Titus 1:7). What is a striker? _____

    _____

    An elder must be a peaceable man.
    C. *Not greedy of filthy lucre* (1 Tim. 3:3; Titus 1:7). How does 1 Peter 5:1-2 relate to this qualification? _____

    _____

    _____

    D. *Not a brawler* (1 Tim. 3:3). Some are not satisfied unless they are in some kind of squabble. Elders need to be able to be differed with and still not get angry and upset.

E. *Not covetous* (1 Tim. 3:3). What does it mean to be covetous?

_____

How would this be damaging to an elder? _____

_____

F. *Not self-willed* (Titus 1:7). How would a person be self-willed?

_____

How is a good way to determine if a man is self-willed? _____

_____

G. *Not soon angry* (Titus 1:7). An elder must not be quick-tempered. Read the advice of Solomon (Prov. 17:14, 27; 22:24; Eccl. 7:9).

VII. Positive Qualifications

A. *Blameless* (1 Tim. 3:2; Titus 1:6). What does it mean to be blameless? _____

_____

This does not mean that an elder is sinless, but that he is a man where no sin can be laid to his charge. He must not do things that disgrace his life as a child of God.

B. *Vigilant* (1 Tim. 3:2). The word "vigilant" carries the idea of

_____

C. *Sober* (1 Tim. 3:2; Titus 1:8). Define the word "sober" as used here. _____

_____

D. *Of good behavior* (1 Tim. 3:2). The behavior of a man reveals what is in his heart (Matt. 12:34). An elder must have his life in order.

E. *Given to hospitality* (1 Tim. 3:2; Titus 1:8). Elders must practice regular hospitality. In fact, they must love it! Read and study 1 Peter 4:9 and Hebrews 13:2.

F. *Patient* (1 Tim. 3:3). What does it mean to be patient? _____

_____

A patient man is not quarrelsome. He is longsuffering.

G. Temperate (Titus 1:8). A man who is an elder must practice self-control. He must be able to hold his temper, tongue, and passions. This would include eating habits!

H. *Lover of good men* (Titus 1:8). Elders must be lovers of what is good. What kind of things will elders promote? _____

_____

_____

They see the good in others and help them develop it to its fullest.

I. *Just* (Titus 1:8). Define the word "just." _____

_____

Notice the message of James 2:1-6; Acts 10:34-35; Romans 2:11; 1 Timothy 5:21.

J. *Holy* (Titus 1:8). A man undefiled by sin and who religiously obeys the Lord. He is devout and practices holiness. Discuss the value of holiness (Heb. 12:14; Rom. 12:1; Eph. 1:4). _____

_____

_____

Conclusion
1. Some thoughts for discussion:
   a. What about "once an elder, always an elder"?_____

_____

   b. Do all of a man's children have to be Christians for him to serve as an elder?_____

   c. Just how important is the wife of an elder? _____

_____

   d. Does a man have to have more than one child to qualify for the eldership?_____

   e. What about a second marriage for an elder? _____

_____

   f. Would a man have to resign the eldership if his wife dies?_____

_____

   g. Why is there a shortage of good, qualified elders? _____

_____

   h. Does the Lord expect much more of elders than He does of any other Christian? _____

_____

2. Only when a man meets all of the qualifications laid down by the Lord can he be Scripturally appointed to the eldership.

Lesson 8

Elders: Shepherds of the Flock (3)

Introduction
1. We continue to study God's place for elders in the local church.
2. In this lesson, we note the importance of leadership, characteristics of good leaders and appointing elders.

Discussion

I. The Importance of Leadership
    A. God has always had those known as His leaders.
        1. Who was the first leader of God's people (Exod. 3:1-18)?

            List some outstanding traits of this leader. _____

        2. Make a list of the outstanding leaders in the Old Testament times and tell what made them so great. _____

    B. A church is no stronger than its leaders!
        1. Paul said that elders are to "_____ well" (1 Tim. 5:17).
        2. The word "rule" here means to lead. Elders are the leaders in the local church.
    C. Describe the situation where no one leads. _____

II. Some Characteristics of a Good Leader

A. A good leader is strong and has courage.

    1. What orders did God give to Joshua as he rose to leadership (Josh. 1:6-9)? _____

       _____

    2. Note David's charge to Solomon (1 Kings 2:1-4). _____

       _____

    3. Elders cannot afford to be afraid to lead.

       a. Some have a melting heart (Josh. 2:11; 7:5).

       b. It is hard for people to take a real stand for truth and against sin when they have a melting heart.

    4. What are some results of being strong and of good courage (Psa. 27:14; 2 Chr. 15:7)? _____

       _____

    5. In the words of Acts 28:15, "Thank God, and take courage."

B. A good leader recognizes the source of his strength.

    1. Paul said, "be _____ in the _____ " (Eph. 6:10).

    2. Too many people depend on their own strength.

C. A good leader realizes that he cannot lead if none are willing to follow.

    1. People cannot be driven, but must be led as sheep.

    2. We need leaders—not drivers!

D. A good leader is not dictatorial.

    1. Elders are not dictators (1 Pet. 5:1-3).

    2. The spirit of Diotrephes is one that will wreck and ruin a good church (3 John 9).

E. A good leader is not jealous.

    1. Some leaders are jealous of other leaders.

    2. Discuss some problems associated with jealousy. _____

       _____

F. A good leader has an understanding heart.

    1. Followers need to be able to talk with men who have understanding.

    2. What did Solomon ask for (1 Kings 3:5-12)? _____

       _____

G. A good leader loves the truth.

    1. Men perish because they do not love the truth (2 Thess. 2:10).

    2. Leaders must love the truth above friendship, popularity, and position.

H. A good leader is just and fears God.
    1. Read and study 2 Samuel 23:1-3.
    2. Leaders of God's people must be just and fair and have respect for God.

I. A good leader will not compromise.
    1. One great thing about Moses was that he would not compromise (Ex. 10:24-26).
    2. We need men who want to please God above men.

J. A good leader will make good use of others.
    1. Good leaders will call on qualified people for help, otherwise they are too limited.
    2. Moses called on others for help (Num. 11:14-17).

K. A good leader has time to do the work.
    1. It takes lots of time to be a good elder.
    2. Time for planning the teaching program, time to convince gainsayers, time to find lost sheep, time to keep up with the attendance and spiritual state of members, time to work with new converts, and time to make plans for the future growth of the church.

L. A good leader knows where he is going.
    1. What happens where there is no vision? _____

    _____
    2. There is a real need for good definite goals for the local church—short term and long term goals. If we aim at nothing, we usually_____ .

M. Study Luke 15:4-7 and John 10:1-18 and list some characteristics of a good shepherd. _____

    _____
    _____

III. Appointing Elders

A. Elders were ordained in every church in New Testament times (Acts 14:23).
B. The exact procedure is a matter of judgment, but they must be appointed.
C. There are several principles to be applied when appointing elders.

1. *Put the church in order* (Titus 1:5). This requires the evangelist teach and preach faithfully on the subject and lead in getting the church properly organized.
2. *Do all things decently and in order* (1 Cor. 14:40). All procedures must be in a decent and well arranged manner.
3. *Do nothing by partiality* (1 Tim. 5:21). Any method that would influence partiality would not conform to this principle.

D. There are three separate steps to be taken in appointing elders.
1. *Determine the qualifications.*
2. *Select the men from among the number.* Whose responsibility is this? _____

_____

3. *Appoint the men to the office.* Who does the appointing?

_____

E. In light of these principles and steps, suggest an orderly fashion for selecting and appointing elders. _____

_____

_____

_____

_____

Conclusion
1. The Bible places great emphasis on appointing good, qualified leaders.
2. What the church will be tomorrow depends a great deal on its leaders today!

Lesson 9

Deacons: Servants of the Church

Introduction

1. The organization of the church includes deacons (Phil. 1:1; 1 Tim. 3:8-13).
2. Deacons serve the Lord's church under the oversight of the elders.

Discussion

I. The Meaning of the Word "Deacon"

    A. The word "deacon" (*diakonos*) means, "one who executes the commands of another, esp. of a master; a servant, attendant, minister" (Thayer, *Greek-English Lexicon of the New Testament*).

    B. For comparison, notice some other words translated "servant."

        1. *Doulos*: "slave, bondman, a man of servile condition" (Thayer).

        2. *Therapon*: "an attendant, servant" (Thayer).

        3. *Huperetes*: "one under power, subordinate power, anyone who serves with his hands; a servant" (Thayer).

    C. Now, in your own words, tell what a deacon is. _____ _____ _____

II. The Qualifications of Deacons

    A. Read and study 1 Timothy 3:8-13.

    B. Negative qualifications:

        1. *Not double tongued* (1 Tim. 3:8).

            a. What does it mean to be double tongued? _____ _____

      b.   How does James 3:8-12 relate to this qualification? ___

          _____

  2. *Not given to much wine* (1 Tim. 3:8).
      a.   Does this give a deacon the right to drink alcoholic beverages? _____

      b.   Defend your answer. _____

          _____

  3. *Not greedy of filthy lucre* (1 Tim. 3:8).
      a.   Discuss what it means to be greedy of filthy lucre. ____

          _____

      b.   How would this be a detriment to the work of a deacon?

          _____

C. Positive qualifications:
  1. *Grave* (1 Tim. 3:8).
      a.   A deacon must be a serious man. One whose life is such that he would be dependable and trustworthy in the work.
      b.   Gravity and sincerity are critical in all aspects of the Lord's work!
  2. *Holding the mystery of the faith in a pure conscience* (1 Tim. 3:9).
      a.   Holding the faith implies stability in the gospel.
      b.   What does it mean to have a pure conscience? _____

          _____

  3. *Husband of one wife* (1 Tim. 3:12).
      a.   Literally, "a one-woman man."
      b.   The nature of his work demands that he be a married man.
  4. *Ruling his children and house well* (1 Tim. 3:12).
      a.   What is the meaning of this qualification? _____

          _____

      b.   What would this suggest about a man? _____

          _____

  5. *First be proved* (1 Tim. 3:10).
      a.   Does the "proving" come before or after deacons are appointed? _____

          _____

      b. How do you think this "proving" is done? _____

    _____

III. The Wives of Deacons
    A. The wives of deacons have an important place.
    B. Read and study 1 Timothy 3:11, and discuss the following terms:
        1. *Grave.* _____
        2. *Not slanderers.* _____
        3. *Sober.* _____
        4. *Faithful in all things.* _____
    C. We must not overlook the wives of officers in the church.

IV. The Work of Deacons
    A. The work of a deacon is suggested in the meaning of the word.
    B. Make a list of things deacons should not do. _____

    _____

    _____

    C. Some things deacons can do:
        1. "Serve tables" (Acts 6:2).
        2. See about the sick and needy.
        3. Prepare bulletins and newsletters.
        4. Check on Bible classes.
        5. Take care of the church building and grounds.
        6. Serve as treasurers.
        7. Arrange the service schedule or work assignments.
        8. Serve the church in any needs.
        9. List other things you can think of. _____

    _____

    _____

    D. Elders need to call on the deacons for help, meet with the deacons routinely, and work up a deacon's schedule. Deacons can be a good source for elders.

Conclusion
1. Compare and contrast the office of a deacon with the office of a bishop.

    _____

2. No congregation is fully developed until it has qualified men appointed to serve as deacons.

Teachers: Teaching Others

Introduction
1. The religion of Jesus Christ is a teaching religion (John 6:44-45).
2. The Lord has set teachers in the church for the purpose of teaching others (Eph. 4:11).

Discussion
I. God's Provision for Teachers
   A. Teaching begins in the home with the parents as teachers.
     1. What does Deuteronomy 6:4-7 say about parents teaching their children? _____

     _____
     2. Ephesians 6:4—"And, ye fathers, provoke not your _____ to wrath: but bring them up in the _____ and _____ of the Lord."
   B. The Lord provided teachers for the church.
     1. Ephesians 4:11—"And he gave some, apostles; and some, prophets; and some, evangelists; and some, pastors and ____ _____."
     2. What were said to be in the church at Antioch (Acts 13:1)?

     _____
   C. The aged women are to teach the young women (Titus 2:3-5). What are aged women to teach young women? _____

   _____

II. The Seriousness of Teaching Others
   A. Teaching others is serious business!
   B. Read and ponder James 3:1.
     1. What is another word for *masters*? _____

2. What is meant by the term *condemnation*? _____

_____

3. What is this passage teaching? _____

_____

C. Write a sentence as to what you think this means: "Don't teach if you can keep from it!" _____

_____

III. The Qualifications of Teachers

A. Do you think there is such a thing as an unqualified teacher?

_____

B. List the two qualifications of teachers from 2 Timothy 2:2 and tell what they mean.

1. _____

2. _____

C. There comes a time when Christians ought to be teachers (Heb. 5:12-14).

IV. Some Responsibilities of Teachers

A. *A teacher must know the truth.*

1. John 8:32—"And ye shall _____ the _____, and the truth shall make you free."

2. A teacher cannot teach that which he or she does not _____.

B. *A teacher must study.*

1. There is no substitute for personal Bible study.

2. Write out and memorize 2 Timothy 2:15. _____

_____

C. *A teacher must spend time in preparation.*

1. Do not wait until the last minute to prepare for teaching.

2. List in order the things Ezra did (Ezra 7:10): _____

_____

D. *A teacher must practice what is taught.*

1. Read and study Romans 2:21-22.

2. A teacher cannot expect his students to do any better than he or she does. Some may need to quit teaching until their _____ catches up with their _____.

V. Some Qualities of a Good Teacher

A. *Enthusiastic.*

1. Read and list the key words of each passage.
   a. Ezekiel 6:11 _____
   b. Acts 8:30 _____
2. What impact will enthusiasm on the part of the teacher have on those who are being taught? _____
_____

B. *Friendly.*
   1. Read and practice Proverbs 18:24.
   2. Learn the names of your students and call them by name.
C. *Optimistic.*
   1. 1 Corinthians 3:6-8
   2. Expect the best—not the worst!
D. *Humble.*
   1. 1 Peter 5:5-6
   2. You do not know-it-all!
E. *Punctual.*
   1. Being on time is important.
   2. Some have a habit of running late all the time.
F. List other qualities you like in a teacher. _____
_____

VI. The Aim of Teaching
A. Teaching others is not without purpose.
B. Read Ephesians 4:12-13 and take note of the aim (purpose) of teaching. _____
_____
C. How does 1 Timothy 4:16 relate to the aim of teaching? _____
_____

VII. Some Things Necessary for Teaching Others
A. *A teacher.* Someone must do the teaching.
B. *Students.* Those who need to be taught.
C. *Curriculum.* Something to be taught.
D. *A place.* Suitable arrangements must be made to facilitate the teaching teacher and the learning listener.

Conclusion
1. Christianity begins and continues through teaching.
2. We need more qualified and effective Bible teachers in the church today!

Lesson 11

Saints: Members At Work

Introduction
1. Paul addressed his Philippian letter, ". . . to all the saints in Christ Jesus which are at Philippi, with the bishops and deacons" (Phil. 1:1).
2. This lesson is a look at the place of saints in the organization of the church.

Discussion

I. What Is a Saint?
    A. A saint is a member of the Lord's church. Paul wrote, "Unto the _____ of God which is at Corinth, to them that are _____ in Christ Jesus, called to be _____ " (1 Cor. 1:2).

    B. The word "saint" describes members of the church as people called out of the world to be God's own people (Acts 9:13; Rom. 1:7; 1 Pet. 2:9-10).

II. As Becometh Saints
    A. When one becomes a saint he belongs to God and must live a consecrated life.

    B. Throughout the Bible, saints are urged to live a life befitting their position.

        1. Romans 16:2 _____

        2. Ephesians 5:1-5 _____

    C. How do Ephesians 4:1 and Colossians 1:10 relate to this? _____
_____
_____

III. Saints Responsibilities to Evangelists
    A. Saints are to receive the word preached by evangelists (1 Thess. 2:13).

B. Saints are to pray for evangelists (Rom. 15:30; 1 Thess. 5:25).

C. Saints are to support evangelists (Phil. 1:5; 4:15-16; Gal. 6:6).

IV. Saints Responsibilities to Elders

A. Saints are to know the elders (1 Thess. 5:12).

B. Saints are to esteem the elders highly in love (1 Thess. 5:13).

C. Saints are to submit unto the elders (Heb. 13:17).

D. Saints are to be at peace (1 Thess. 5:13).

E. Saints are to obey the elders (Heb. 13:17).

F. Saints are to call the elders in time of need (Jas. 5:14).

V. Saints Responsibilities in the Local Church

A. Saints are required to assemble to worship God (Heb. 10:25).

B. Saints should be able to teach others (Heb. 5:12; 2 Tim. 2:2).

C. Saints are to be members at work (1 Cor. 15:58; Heb. 6:10).

D. Saints should visit the sick, help the distressed, and know how to answer every man (Jas. 1:27; Col. 4:6).

E. Saints should work together for the building up of the body of Christ (1 Cor. 12:25; Eph. 4:16).

VI. Saints Responsibilities to One Another

A. Saints responsibilities to one another from a negative standpoint:
   1. Saints must NOT do wrong one to another (Acts 7:23-29).
   2. Saints must NOT be puffed up for one against another (1 Cor. 4:6).
   3. Saints must NOT go to law one with another (1 Cor. 6:7).
   4. Saints must NOT bite and devour one another (Gal. 5:15).
   5. Saints must NOT provoke and envy one another (Gal. 5:26).
   6. Saints must NOT lie to one another (Col. 3:9; Eph. 4:25).
   7. Saints must NOT speak evil of one another (Jas. 4:11).
   8. Saints must NOT grudge against one another (Jas. 5:9).

B. Saints responsibilities to one another from a positive standpoint:
   1. Saints must love one another (John 13:34-35; 1 Pet. 1:22).
   2. Saints must be of the same mind toward one another (Rom. 12:16).
   3. Saints must edify one another (Rom. 14:19).
   4. Saints must admonish one another (Rom. 15:14).
   5. Saints must greet one another (2 Cor. 13:12).
   6. Saints must care for one another (1 Cor. 12:25-26).

7. Saints must serve one another (Gal. 5:13).
8. Saints must bear one another's burdens (Gal. 6:2).
9. Saints must forbear one another (Eph. 4:2; Col. 3:13).
10. Saints must forgive one another (Eph. 4:32).
11. Saints must submit to one another (Eph. 5:21).
12. Saints must comfort one another (1 Thess. 4:18).
13. Saints must exhort one another (Heb. 10:25).
14. Saints must confess their faults to one another (Jas. 5:16).
15. Saints must pray for one another (Jas. 5:16).
16. Saints must use hospitality toward one another (1 Pet. 4:9-10).

Conclusion
1. Each saint has a part to supply in the organization of the church (1 Cor. 12:12-25).
2. Every saint is important and must fulfill his place in the organization of the Lord's church.

Problems: Abuses of Organization

Introduction

1. Down through the years, problems have crept up in the organization of the church.
2. In the first century, Paul warned of abuses of organization (Acts 20:28-31; 2 Thess. 2:2-4).
3. Let's notice some abuses of organization that have occurred in the church.

Discussion

I. A Distinction Made Between Elders and Bishops

    A. In the second century, there was a gradual distinction made between elders and bishops.

        1. One of the elders in a congregation began to be regarded as a leader of the others. This "leading elder" or "the bishop" in a congregation located in an important city came to have authority over others in his area.

        2. Such a distinction led to a "Universal Bishop" in 595 A.D. and a man being crowned Pope, head of the church on earth, in 606 A.D.

        3. This abuse of organization brought about an apostasy from the Lord's church and gave rise to the Roman Catholic Church.

    B. Does the Bible make a distinction between an elder and a bishop (Acts 20:17, 28; Titus 1:5, 7; 1 Pet. 5:1-2)? _____

    C. How much authority does one elder have over another elder?

_____

II. Missionary Societies in the Work of Evangelism

A. Brethren have built and maintained human organizations to do the work of evangelism.

B. On October 24, 1849, the American Christian Missionary Society was formed in Cincinnati, Ohio. Alexander Campbell was elected president.

C. Here is the way the missionary society works: Churches send funds to the missionary society. The missionary society board directs the work and takes charge of the funds raised by contributing churches.

D. Did any church in the New Testament ever send money to a missionary society to do any of its work (2 Cor. 11:8-9; Phil. 4:15-16)? _____

E. The missionary society is an abuse of the organization of the church.

III. The Sponsoring Church Arrangement

A. A sponsoring church is a church that sponsors a work greater than its ability and receives money from other churches to accomplish that work.

B. Many churches today send to one church which is known as the "sponsoring church." The elders of this church oversee the work (select the preacher, the field of work, etc.), while other churches furnish the money.

C. Sponsoring churches are trying to do a work larger than the local church. Putting such a work under an eldership where they receive the funds from other churches does not change the abuse!

D. Examples of sponsoring church arrangements include "One Nation Under God" and "The Herald of Truth."

E. Be ready to discuss how the sponsoring church arrangement is an abuse of organization, and provide the passages. _____
_____
_____

IV. Benevolent Societies in the Work of Benevolence

A. Today, churches are sending funds to a benevolent society such as Orphan's Homes and Old Folk's Homes, and the benevolent society provides the place, provisions, and personnel in the work of benevolence or relief.

B. The New Testament authorizes three possibilities for the benevolent work of the church.
   1. *The church may care for its own needy* (Acts 2:44-45; 4:32-35; 6:1-8).
   2. *The church may send funds to other churches to supply the needs of the saints* (Acts 11:27-30).
   3. *Several churches may send to one church* (1 Cor. 16:1-3; 2 Cor. 8:1-5; 9:1-2; Rom. 15:25-32).
C. When one church sent funds to another church, the funds were always sent directly to the church in need. There was no organization between the sending church and the receiving church.
D. The local church has been charged with the responsibility of preaching the gospel and helping needy saints. It does not have the right to turn any of its work over to any human organization. To do so would constitute an abuse of organization.

V. Women in Positions of Leadership in the Church
A. The organization of the church is abused when women are placed in positions of leadership in the church.
B. Today, there are women preachers, elders, deacons, song leaders, etc.
C. How do 1 Corinthians 14:34 and 1 Timothy 2:11-15 limit the role of women in the church? _____

   _____

   _____

D. Discuss some things women can do which are not an abuse of organization. _____

   _____

   _____

   _____

VI. Committees and Organizations Within the Local Church
A. Local church organization is abused when organizations smaller than the local church are formed to function independently of the church.
B. Such organizations are Sunday school organizations, Ladies' Aid Societies, Young People's Societies, and committees which have their presidents, superintendents, treasuries and the like which function separate and independent of the church.

The Organization of the Church ‖‖‖‖‖‖‖‖‖‖‖‖‖‖‖‖‖‖‖‖‖‖‖‖‖‖‖‖‖‖‖‖ **45**

C. How are these an abuse of organization? _____

_____
_____
_____

Conclusion
1. These abuses of organization keep folks from understanding the New Testament pattern for the organization of the church.
2. When the organization of the church is abused, apostasy is just around the bend!

Conclusion: Keeping the Church Pure in Organization

Introduction
1. Every Christian must guard the purity of church organization.
2. Here are some ways we can keep the church pure in organization:

Discussion
I. **Each Church Organized after the New Testament Pattern**
   A. In this series of Bible studies, we have noticed the New Testament pattern for the organization of the church.
   B. Discuss the New Testament pattern for the organization of the church, in light of this study. _____
   _____
   _____
   _____

   C. There are many churches today that simply are not organized after the New Testament pattern, and this destroys the purity of the church!
   D. If the church is to be kept pure in organization, every one of us must insist that each church be organized properly.

II. **Each Church Plans Its Own Work**
   A. The local church must exercise vision in planning its own work of evangelism, edification, and benevolence.
   B. Many times this is not done. There are churches that function simply to help execute the plans of other churches. There are churches that have their work outlined for them by boards and outside elderships.

C. How would each church planning its own work guard the purity of church organization? _____

_____

_____

D. Which church in the New Testament planned the work of another church, and which church let another church plan its work?

_____

Provide the Scripture. _____

III. Each Church Does Its Own Work Under Supervision of Its Own Elders

A. In New Testament times, each church did its own work. There is not a single example of a church turning over any of its work to another church or organization.

B. There are churches failing to do their own work. Many churches would rather send their money to another church or a society and let them in turn do their work for them.

C. Do you think each church is capable of doing its own work?

_____

D. Show from the Scriptures that each church must do its own work. _____

_____

_____

_____

IV. Each Church Disciplines Its Own Members

A. God has charged each church with the responsibility of discipline.

B. Read the following passages and write the key words about discipline in the church.
   1. 1 Corinthians 5:1-13 _____
   2. 2 Thessalonians 3:6-15 _____
   3. Titus 3:10-11 _____

C. Discipline in the church is the Lord's way of keeping His church pure.

V. Each Church Cares for Its Own Needy Members

A. The work of the local church involves taking care of its own needy.
   1. 1 Timothy 5:16—"If any man or woman that believeth have

widows, let them relieve them, and let not the church be charged; that it may _____ them that are _____ indeed."

    2. Read the following passages and note the example of the Jerusalem church in caring for its own members.

       a. Acts 2:44-45 _____

       b. Acts 4:34-35 _____

       c. Acts 6:1-6 _____

B. Many times instead of each church caring for its own needy, churches send their needy members to other churches or organizations to be cared for. They may pay their keep, but in most cases they expect others to do it.

VI. Each Church Makes Its Own Decisions in Matters of Expediency

A. There are some areas in which the Lord has left it up to the church to decide its own course of action.

    1. The Lord has commanded us to assemble on the first day of the week (Acts 20:7; Heb. 10:25), but has left it to us to decide the time and place.

    2. The Lord has authorized the church to preach the gospel (1 Thess. 1:8), but has given room for us to make our own decisions as to the means of doing the work.

    3. The Lord has given the church responsibility in caring for its own needy members (1 Cor. 16:1-3), but the church may decide the place, the provisions, and the personnel.

    4. The Lord has commanded the church to engage in the work of edification (Eph. 4:12-16), but the church is free to decide the place, the time, and the arrangements.

B. Each church needs to make its own decisions in these areas. We violate the autonomy of the local church if we allow other churches to set the precedent for us.

VII. Each Church Takes Full Control of Its Own Resources

A. The only means of financing the Lord's work is through the collection taken up on the first day of the week (1 Cor. 16:1-2).

B. Each church must oversee the expenditure of its own funds, rather than allowing some other church or organization to do it for them.

The Organization of the Church

C. How would this be a safety measure for the church? _____

_____

_____

D. Can you find an example in the New Testament where one church allowed another church to control its resources? _____

Conclusion

1. Every generation must take care to keep the church of our Lord pure in organization!

2. May each of us who make up the church find his place in the organization of the church, get in that place, and stay in it!

Materials Available From the Edwards Family

- *Home Bible Study* (Four lesson series for truth seekers. Available in English, Russian & Spanish)
- *Home Bible Study on DVD* (Audio/video presentation of the four lesson Home Bible Study)
- *Home Bible Study Correspondence Course* (Four lesson correspondence course for truth seekers)
- *Growing in Grace and Knowledge of the Lord* (Thirteen lesson series for new converts and growing Christians)
- *Locating the Lord's Church* (Thirteen lesson series for truth seekers and growing Christians)
- *Men's Training Class* (Eight lesson series for the men of the church)
- *The Organization of the Church* (Thirteen lesson series for truth seekers and growing Christians)
- *The Two Covenants* (Thirteen lesson series for truth seekers and growing Christians)
- *Gospel Sermons by Three Generations of Preachers* (One hundred sermon outlines reflecting over one hundred years of study and preaching)
- *The Family and the Home* (Thirteen lesson series for truth seekers and growing Christians)
- *Bible Baptism* (Thirteen lesson series for truth seekers and growing Christians)
- *Be Strong in the Lord* (Thirteen lesson series for truth seekers and growing Christians)
- *Answering Religious Error* (Handbook and class study guide containing simple Bible answers to many complex religious errors)
- *Older Women Admonish the Young Women* (Thirteen lesson series for ladies Bible classes)
- *Women Professing Godliness* (Eight lesson series for ladies Bible classes)
- *Soul Winning Tool Kit* (Contains an eight lesson study book and tools for doing personal work)
- *What Saith the Scripture?* (Three volume collection of religious writings)
- *Let Us Rise Up and Build* (Eight lesson series for building Christians)

www.ingramcontent.com/pod-product-compliance
Lightning Source LLC
Chambersburg PA
CBHW071744020426
42331CB00008B/2161